Ortho Easy-Step Books

Lawns

*Created and designed
by the editorial staff of
Ortho Books*

Contents

A lawn is often the central and largest portion of a home landscape. For an attractive, healthy, and long-lasting lawn, you will need to select the right grass for your climate and needs, install it properly with careful attention to preparing the planting bed, and care for it consistently. This book will show you how. Whether you are starting from scratch and planting a new lawn where none existed, or removing and replanting an old or neglected lawn, or just looking for clear and concise lawn-care information, you will find it in the pages that follow.

Check the Table of Contents on pages 2 and 3. All the steps to a beautiful lawn are laid out there. Each step is described and illustrated in an easy-to-follow way to make the job go quickly and smoothly. And should you encounter pest or disease problems, information on identifying and solving them is included. The final section of the book provides some background information on different grass types, seed selection, and mowing heights.

Anatomy of a Grass Plant

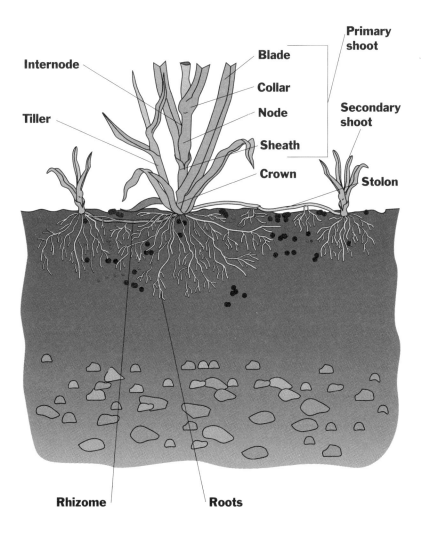

Planting a Lawn

1 Clear the site

Remove all debris such as wood, stones, large roots, and weeds or old sod from the planting area. Do not bury any debris under the future lawn and check for any a builder may have left. Don't mix old sod into the soil. Remove weeds with a hoe or shovel, or spray them with an herbicide such as glyphosate. Some weedy grasses need to be sprayed two or more times at two-week intervals. An old lawn can be removed by hand or with a mechanical sod cutter (available at most equipment-rental stores) after it has been killed with an herbicide.

Remove old turf and discard.

Remove rocks and debris.

2

Establish a rough grade

The purpose of rough grading is to remove or add enough soil to bring the soil surface to the height and slope necessary to ensure proper drainage. Grade soil so there is a smooth, gradual slope away from any buildings. The ground within 6 feet of a foundation should drop ¾ inch for each foot of distance. Use a string attached to a pair of stakes to check the grade. Adjust the string so it is level. Measure down from the string at 1-foot intervals to determine the existing slope.

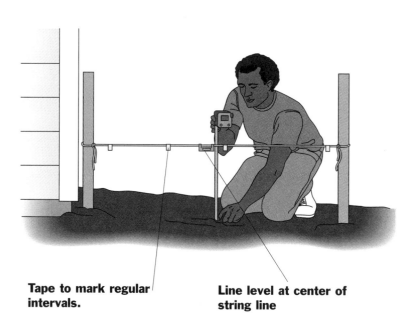

Tape to mark regular intervals.

Line level at center of string line

Add or remove soil as necessary and rake to shape the final grade. If you plan to lay sod, allow for its thickness. Avoid adding or removing more than 2 inches of soil under large trees. When an underlying layer of impenetrable soil or heavy clay soil inhibits drainage, you may need to install drain lines and catch basins. Consult a drainage contractor for advice. Drainage work should be done after the rough grading but before adding topsoil and amendments.

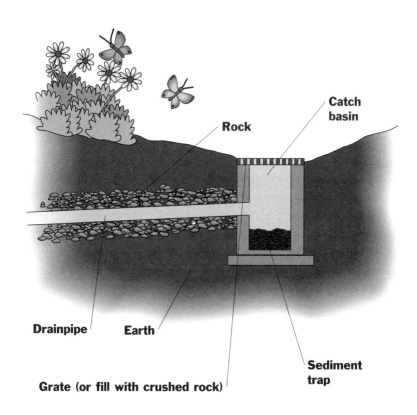

Rock

Catch basin

Drainpipe   **Earth**

Grate (or fill with crushed rock)

Sediment trap

3 Prepare the soil

Dig up and turn over the graded soil with a shovel, spade, or a rotary tiller to a depth of 8 to 12 inches before adding amendments. Use amendments to help change the texture, pH, and nutrient content of the soil. Organic matter such as compost or finely ground fir bark will improve clay, sandy, or loam soils. Gypsum, lime, or sulfur can be added to clay soils. A fertilizer high in phosphorus (see page 31) will get the lawn off to a good start. Adding amendments will raise the level of the existing soil. Remove some soil first.

Churn soil 8" to 12" deep.

Add soil amendments and fertilizer.

Spread the amendments and fertilizer on the surface and work in to a depth of 6 to 8 inches. Rake and level the soil. Install an underground sprinkler system or edging at this point. Use a lawn roller half-filled with water to firm the soil and help reveal areas that need further leveling. The prepared soil should be ½ inch lower than sidewalks and driveways if planting seed, plugs, or sprigs, and 1 to 2 inches lower for sod. Make sure the soil is as smooth and finely ground as possible before planting.

Work in amendments and fertilizer.

Rake and level.

Smooth with roller.

4 Choose the right grass type

Choose a grass that suits the climate, soil type, amount of use, shade, and maintenance it will encounter. Grasses are categorized as either cool-season or warm-season (see below). Cool-season grasses grow best where summers are warm and winters cold and in mild coastal areas. Warm-season grasses are best adapted to areas with hot summers and mild winters, and will often stay green all year in the southeastern United States. In other areas, they go dormant and turn brown when cold weather arrives.

Lawn Grass Comparisons—Warm-Season Grasses

	Bahiagrass	Common bermudagrass	Hybrid bermudagrass
Establishment speed	○	●	●
Heat tolerance	●	●	●
Cold tolerance	○	○	○
Drought tolerance	○	●	●
Shade tolerance	○	○	○

● = Good   ○ = Moderate   ○ = Poor

Warm-Season Grasses (continued)

	Centipede-grass	St. Augustine grass	Zoysiagrass
Establishment speed	○	○	○
Heat tolerance	●	●	●
Cold tolerance	○	○	○
Drought tolerance	○	○	●
Shade tolerance	○	●	●

● = Good   ○ = Moderate   ○ = Poor

Buy high-quality seed, sod, sprigs, or plugs from reputable companies and choose the planting method that best suits your needs. Using seed is the least expensive way of starting a lawn, and you'll find a wide variety of types to choose from. Seeded lawns require intensive maintenance until established, however. Sod provides an "instant lawn" but is more expensive. Sprigs and plugs are less costly than sod but require lots of work to install and take a while to fill in completely.

Lawn Grass Comparisons—Cool-Season Grasses

	Creeping bentgrass	Kentucky bluegrass	Rough bluegrass
Establishment speed	○	○	○
Heat tolerance	○	○	○
Cold tolerance	●	●	●
Drought tolerance	○	○	○
Shade tolerance	○	○	●

● = Good   ○ = Moderate   ○ = Poor

Cool-Season Grasses (continued)

	Fine fescues	Tall fescues	Annual ryegrass	Perennial ryegrass
Establishment speed	○	○	●	●
Heat tolerance	○	○	○	○
Cold tolerance	●	○	○	○
Drought tolerance	○	●	○	○
Shade tolerance	●	●	○	○

● = Good   ○ = Moderate   ○ = Poor

5 Plant with seed

Sow seed on a calm day and spread it evenly at the rate recommended on the package. Split the appropriate quantity of seed in half and spread the second half at right angles to the first. Use a handheld, drop, or broadcast spreader for even coverage, touching up the edges of the lawn as needed. Rake lightly in one direction to mix the seed only into the top ⅛ to ¼ inch of soil.

Spread seed twice—the second pass at right angles to the first.

Rake lightly in one direction.

Apply top dressing.

To help conserve moisture and keep birds from eating the seeds, apply a thin layer of weed-free organic matter such as compost or a commercially packaged top dressing. Use a lawn roller to press the seed into contact with the soil. String and flag the area to keep people off. Thoroughly soak the soil after planting and keep it moist at all times. Sprinkle as often as four times a day until the young grass is established.

Press seed into the soil with a half-filled roller.

T I P : Deter birds with aluminum pie plates hung with wire from wooden stakes so the plates will blow in the wind.

Keep the soil moist.

6 Plant with sod

Decide on the appropriate variety of sod and determine the square footage of the area to be planted (see page 54). Order the sod about one week before the planting date. When it arrives, stack the pallets in a cool, shaded area and keep the exposed soil moist. Lay sod within 24 hours on slightly moist soil, beginning next to a straight edge such as a sidewalk or driveway. If the lawn area is irregularly shaped, draw a straight line through it or string a line across it and start laying sod on either side of the line.

In an irregularly shaped lawn, string a line and begin laying sod on either side. Place each roll tightly against the previous strip.

Place the loose end of the next roll tightly against the end of the previous strip and carefully unroll it. Use your fingers to firm the joints, but do not stretch the sod. Stagger the ends of the strips in a bricklike pattern. Use a sharp knife to cut along edges and around curves and sprinkler heads. Water the newly laid sod, then roll it with a lawn roller at right angles to how it was laid. Keep it moist and undisturbed for two to four weeks or longer until you feel resistance when you tug gently at a corner.

1. Cut sod around sprinkler heads, trees, and curves.
2. Roll to press roots against soil.
3. Keep the finished lawn moist until the sod knits with the soil beneath.

Plant with sprigs or plugs

Plant sprigs from late spring to midsummer. With a hoe, dig 2- to 3-inch deep furrows spaced from 4 to 12 inches apart. Place the sprigs in the furrows so that the foliage is above ground and the light-colored stems below ground. Firm the soil around each stem and level the area. Roll the planted area with a half-filled lawn roller and water immediately. A sprigged lawn takes two months to two years to fill in, depending on the grass variety and the spacing of the sprigs.

Sprig

1. Cut furrows 2" to 3" deep in prepared soil.

2. Place sprigs 4" to 12" apart. Firm soil around each stem.

3. Roll the planted area and keep it moist.

Plant plugs just as spring weather begins. Use a steel plugger, a trowel, or small shovel to make holes 1 inch wider and deeper than the plugs themselves. Space the holes 6 to 12 inches apart, depending on the size of the plugs and type of grass. Set the plugs in a checkerboard pattern. Firm the soil around them so that the points where the leaf blades and soil meet are level with the ground. Roll and water the plugs, keeping them moist until they are well established.

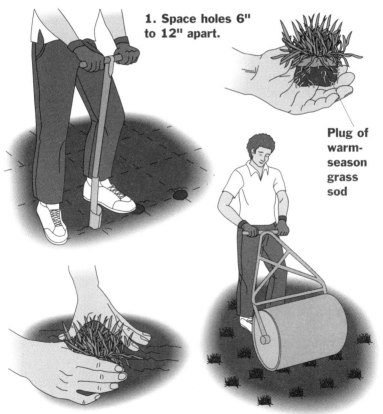

1. Space holes 6" to 12" apart.

Plug of warm-season grass sod

2. Plant plugs and firm the soil around them.

3. Roll the planted area and keep it moist.

Choose a mower

The two most common types of lawn mowers are the gas-powered or manual push *reel* and the gas or electrically powered *rotary*. The power rotary mower is the most popular. Its blades cut like a spinning scythe, useful for taller, less intensively maintained lawns. Reel mowers are preferred for finely cut lawns. When buying a mower, consider the starting system, maneuverability, and means for adjusting handle and cutting height. Make sure the grass catcher is easy to put on and take off, and ask about the safety features.

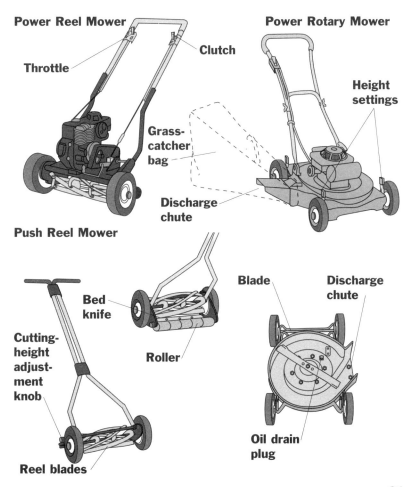

Power Reel Mower

Throttle

Clutch

Power Rotary Mower

Height settings

Grass-catcher bag

Discharge chute

Push Reel Mower

Bed knife

Cutting-height adjustment knob

Roller

Reel blades

Blade

Discharge chute

Oil drain plug

Know how and when to mow

The type of grass, season of year, and overall quality of care it receives will dictate how often you should mow the lawn. Cool-season grasses need to be mowed more often in spring, fall, and winter (in areas without snow), and less often in summer. Warm-season grasses grow fairly slowly in late fall, winter, and spring, but need more frequent mowing in summer and early fall. Mow when the grass grows about one-third taller than its recommended mowing height (see page 58).

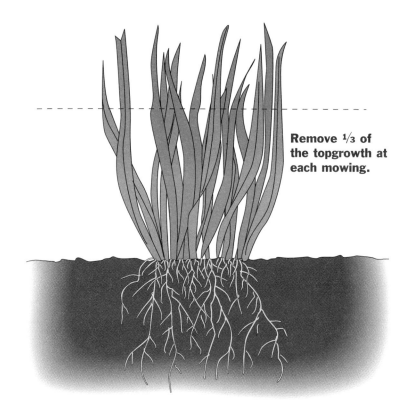

Remove ⅓ of the topgrowth at each mowing.

- Clear the lawn of sticks, stones, and other debris before mowing.
- Start a power mower on a level surface.
- To be safe, push a rotary mower forward; don't pull it backward.
- Don't mow wet grass. It cuts unevenly, and the clippings can mat and block light from the grass.
- Vary the mowing pattern so ruts don't form.
- Mow slopes at a slight diagonal.
- Always stop the engine before leaving a power mower.

Adjust height of mower at each wheel.

Trim and edge

Trimming (cutting stray high blades) and edging (grooming the lawn's edges by cutting alongside them) can be done manually with grass shears and an edger or with gasoline- or electrically powered equipment. The popular string trimmer cuts with a nylon filament that rotates rapidly at the end of a long handle. Wear goggles to protect against flying debris and be careful not to damage the trunks of trees. To save time and energy, trim and edge a lawn first and then pick up the clippings while mowing.

Edger

String trimmer

Recycle the grass clippings

When a lawn is mowed often, leaving the short clippings on the grass to decompose can be both timesaving and beneficial. Long clippings can be a problem, however, if they mat down and block light from the lawn. Mulching mowers are rotary types without a discharge chute or with one that can be closed. The clippings are cut several times into small pieces underneath the mower and then fall into the lawn, where they decompose. Clippings from a regular mower can be composted or used as mulch elsewhere in the garden.

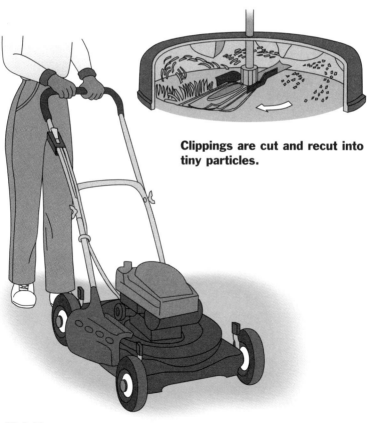

Clippings are cut and recut into tiny particles.

Mulching mower

Wat_ing and F_rtilizing

1 Know when to water

Early morning is usually the best time to water, because of less wind, milder temperatures, and adequate water pressure. How often to water depends on what kind of grass and soil you have, what the weather is like, and what pattern of watering you have established (lawns are often overwatered). It is best to soak the soil deeply and not water again until the top inch or two begins to dry out. Watered this way, roots extend deep into the soil, helping the lawn live through longer periods of drought.

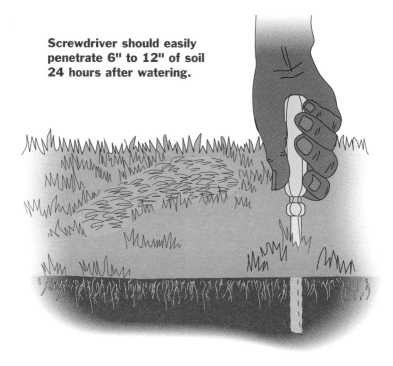

Screwdriver should easily penetrate 6" to 12" of soil 24 hours after watering.

Signs of a thirsty lawn include a lighter-than-normal green color, or grass blades that fold or stay down after being walked on.

Select a sprinkler

Underground sprinkler systems are convenient and efficient and are best installed before a new lawn is planted. They can be added to an existing one, but the lawn will need repairing afterward. Portable sprinklers can also be used; they include the stationary, oscillating-arm, whirling-head, and impulse types. Choose the one that will best cover the area where it is to be used. Different brands of the same type of sprinkler may distribute water in very different patterns, so be aware of how your sprinkler works.

Spray Patterns

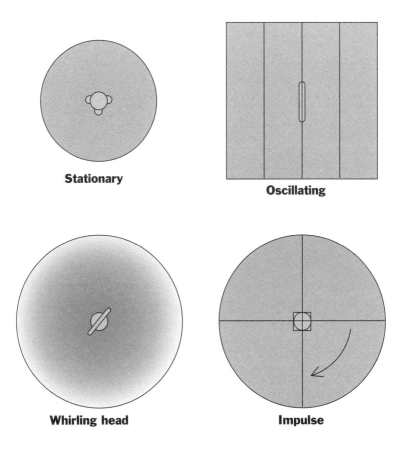

Stationary

Oscillating

Whirling head

Impulse

The stationary type of hose-end sprinkler consists of a small metal or plastic chamber pierced with holes that spray water in a fixed pattern. These are useful for small areas. Oscillating-arm sprinklers have an arched, perforated pipe that sweeps back and forth to deliver water in a rectangular pattern. The whirling-head sprinkler has two or more rotating arms that spray jets of water in a circular pattern. Impulse (or impact) sprinklers deliver pulses of water in a part- to full-circle pattern and are best for large areas.

Stationary sprinkler. Has a small pattern and a high precipitation rate. Best for spot watering.

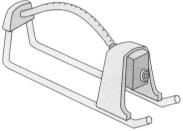

Oscillating-arm sprinkler. Rectangular pattern, usually very even.

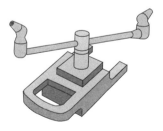

Whirling-head sprinkler. May give uneven coverage. Each nozzle can be adjusted separately.

Impulse sprinkler. Best for large areas. Can be adjusted to water part circle or full circle.

Measure the water distribution

To get a good idea of the sprinkler pattern and amount of water distributed, set up a gridlike arrangement of small containers of the same size on a section of the lawn, extending them at set intervals from the sprinkler head outward. Turn on the sprinkler at the normal operating pressure, leave it on for a set period of time, then observe the amount of water deposited in each container. An inch of water should be adequate. Adjust the sprinkler type and placement and the duration of watering accordingly.

Gridlike arrangement of small containers to test water distribution

Choose the right fertilizer

A lawn will have best overall health and vigor if given a complete fertilizer containing nitrogen, phosphorus, and potassium at least twice a year, preferably in the spring and fall (more often in some regions and with some grass types). High-nitrogen fertilizers stimulate top growth, whereas those higher in phosphorus and potassium also encourage root growth, cell division, and disease resistance. Iron helps give the lawn a dark green color. Read labels carefully to determine which is best for your lawn.

The *grade* or *formula* indicates the percentages of nitrogen, phosphoric acid, and potash—in that order.
A list of all the nutrients and the amount of each is shown in the *analysis.*

5 Apply lawn food correctly

The most common methods of applying fertilizer are spraying, broadcast spreading, and drop spreading. Use a sprayer to apply a liquid or water-soluble powdered fertilizer, and either a broadcast or drop spreader to apply a dry, granular fertilizer. (Spreaders can be purchased or rented from nurseries.) Always fill sprayers or spreaders over a sidewalk or driveway. If some concentrated fertilizer is spilled on the lawn, hose it away or scrape it up, then flood the area with water to avoid fertilizer burn.

Spread dry fertilizer with a drop or handheld broadcast spreader. Overlap about 1/4 on each pass for even coverage.

To apply liquid fertilizer with a hose-end sprayer, measure the concentrated product into the sprayer container and fill it with water to the proper level. Apply the entire contents of the sprayer onto the lawn, covering it evenly. For large lawns, use a broadcast spreader. Walk at a normal speed, keep the spreader level, and overlap passes by about one fourth their width. Use a drop spreader on small- to medium-sized lawns. Overlap the width of one wheel so that no strips are left underfertilized, but be careful not to double-feed any sections.

Overlap the wheel tracks for even coverage.

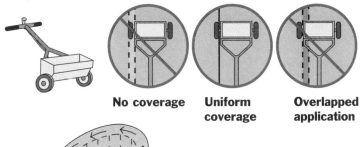

No coverage   Uniform   Overlapped
                 coverage   application

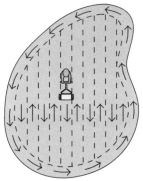

For an irregular shape, apply a header strip around it. Then go back and forth the long way, shutting off the spreader at the header strip.

Shut off the spreader when you reach the header strip and any trees or other obstacles.

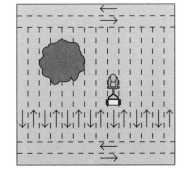

Controlling Problems

Inspect for pests

Look for pests on the edge of a damaged area. Part the grass with your fingers and watch for pest movement or droppings. Use soapy water in a bottomless can placed on the lawn to detect insects feeding in the root zone. If the grass can be rolled back like carpet, numerous grubs are present. Grass plants that pull out at their crowns, exposing a sawdustlike material, have been damaged by billbug larvae. Properly identify pest type and number before applying any treatment.

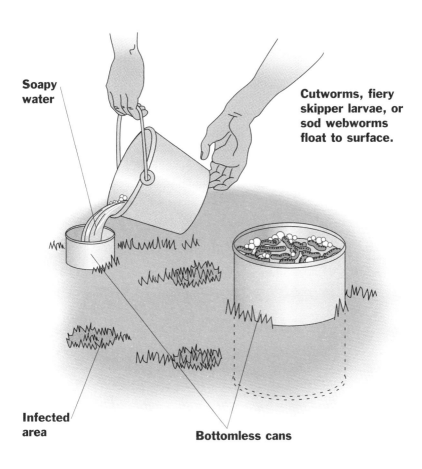

Soapy water

Cutworms, fiery skipper larvae, or sod webworms float to surface.

Infected area

Bottomless cans

Treat insect damage

For help with pest identification and to determine proper treatment, take a sample of the damaged lawn, including a section of top growth and roots, in a sealed container to a qualified person at a local nursery, or to the nearest county Agricultural Extension office. Apply pesticides only after careful diagnosis of the problem and when there are enough harmful insects present to cause damage. Always read the label before purchasing a product and follow all directions carefully.

Safe Pesticide Use

- Pesticides are toxic and can harm beneficial bees, butterflies, and birds. Use only when a definite need has been established.
- Do not overuse pesticides. This may increase resistance in the pests you are attempting to eradicate.
- Do not mix pesticides and do not add them to other lawn chemicals.
- Keep pesticides away from streams and other water supplies.
- Keep children and pets off a treated lawn until the pesticide has dried—at least 24 hours (more in damp weather).
- Spray contact pesticides in the late afternoon or early evening.
- Avoid spraying on a windy day. Wash off cars, lawn furniture, or other outdoor equipment immediately if pesticides land on them.
- Do not mow the lawn for at least 48 hours after applying a pesticide.
- Do not spray pesticides when the temperature exceeds 85° F.
- Store chemicals out of reach of children, in their original, labeled containers.
- Keep pesticides in a locked cabinet—out of direct sunlight and where temperatures will stay cool.

Pesticides for lawns exist in two forms: sprays, applied with a hose-end sprayer; and granules, distributed with a broadcast or drop spreader. If treating for insects feeding on aboveground grass parts, water thoroughly first, since the chemicals can damage drought-stressed grasses, then do not water for 48 hours. For underground pests, water right after spraying, to flush the pesticide into the soil. Apply granules when the lawn is wet.

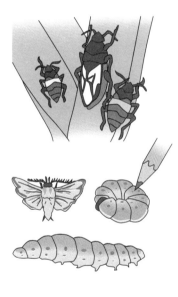

Lawn pests above ground—chinch bugs, leafhoppers, spider mites, and similar pests. To control: Mow, then water heavily. When grass is dry, apply pesticide according to label. Don't water for 48 hours.

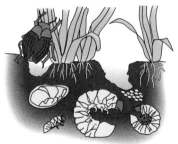

Lawn pests at soil surface—armyworms, cutworms, fiery skipper larvae, and sod webworms. To control: Mow, then water heavily. When grass is dry, apply pesticide according to label (late afternoon is best). Don't water for 48 hours.

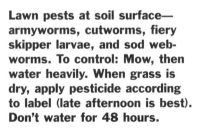

Lawn pests below ground—ground pearls, grubs (beetle larvae), and wireworms. To control: Apply pesticide according to label directions, then water heavily, but not so much that the pesticide washes away.

 Control weed growth

The best way to control weeds is by maintaining a healthy, dense lawn. Avoid over- or under-watering, fertilize only as needed, and mow to the proper height. Soil compaction, poor drainage, too much shade, or excessive wear can also create conditions where weeds will move in. Weeds can be removed by hand or with a weeding tool. Be sure to pull out the entire weed—roots as well as the tops. Hand-weeding takes time and effort but avoids the need for a chemical herbicide.

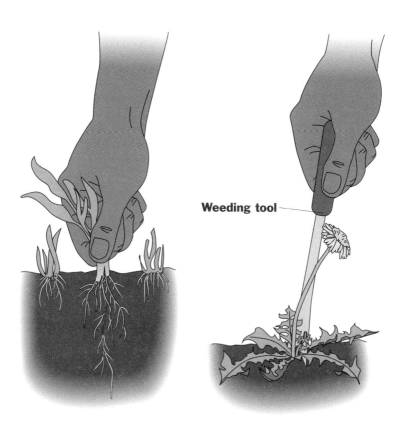

Weeding tool

Prevent weed seed germination

Use a preemergent herbicide to prevent weeds from invading an existing lawn. Liquid and granular forms are equally effective. These herbicides last 6 to 12 weeks and form a chemical barrier near the soil surface that kills seeds before weeds emerge. Don't apply to a newly seeded lawn—the chemical could kill it. Apply to an established lawn one to two weeks before weed seeds begin to germinate: in early spring just as the soil begins to warm up, and again in early fall.

Apply liquid form with a tank-type or hose-end sprayer.

Apply granular forms using a handheld broadcast spreader or a push-type drop or broadcast spreader.

Eliminate existing weeds

Apply a postemergent herbicide to kill growing weeds that are too plentiful to eliminate by hand. Contact herbicides kill only aboveground plant parts that are covered by the chemical. Systemic herbicides kill all parts of the plant. Selective types kill one kind of plant but not another. Do not use herbicides on a new lawn until it has grown enough to need three mowings. Read labels carefully and follow all instructions exactly.

Burclover
Control with a post-emergent herbicide in fall or spring, or hand-weed in small lawns.

Dandelion
Spray in early spring and early fall with a post-emergent herbicide.

Oxalis
Treat with preemergent controls in early spring, or postemergents in spring or fall. Several treatments may be necessary.

Plantain
Cut out clumps so that no roots remain, or spot-treat in spring or fall before the flower spikes form.

Herbicides usually work best on young, succulent, actively growing weeds, and when the soil is moist and warm. (In the Southeast, treat bermudagrass lawns during the hot, humid months; St. Augustine grass in late fall or early winter.) Do not spray on windy days or when it is warmer than 80° F. Don't mow right before applying an herbicide or for two days afterward. If possible, spot-treat weeds rather than apply the chemical over the entire lawn. Avoid getting the herbicide on nearby plants, and don't use a container that has held an herbicide for any other purpose.

Spotted Spurge
Use a preemergent herbicide in early spring and again in midsummer. Control young plants with a postemergent product.

Annual Bluegrass
Use preemergent controls in early August through early October, or spot-treat with a post-emergent and reseed.

Bermudagrass
No preemergent controls available. Use a post-emergent in fall or early spring. Repeat treatment if needed.

Crabgrass
Use preemergent controls in spring, but not on bentgrass, centi-pedegrass, or St. Augustine grass. Use postemergent controls when weeds are small.

6 Control diseases

Most lawn diseases are caused by parasitic plants called fungi that spread by microscopic spores. Planting a grass appropriate for the climate, watering in the morning rather than at night, and maintaining the lawn well will help prevent diseases. If they do take hold, they can be controlled with fungicides—either contact or systemic. Contact fungicides work on the outside of plants and are best used before diseases start. Systemic fungicides work from inside plants and are usually the most effective type.

Brown Patch (Rhizoctonia Blight)
Prevent by reducing shade and thatch, watering deeply, and aerating the lawn. Limit applications of nitrogen-rich fertilizers.

Fairy Ring
Keep the lawn healthy. Aerate the rings; increase water penetration by using a wetting agent in the ring area.

Fusarium Patch
Prevent through shade reduction, aeration, and improved drainage. Cut back on fall fertilizing. Treat with fungicides in the late fall.

Leaf Spot
Control with appropriate fungicides. To prevent, avoid over-fertilizing in spring, improve aeration and drainage, reduce shade, and mow properly.

Both contact and systemic fungicides are available as granules that are spread, as powders that are mixed with water for spraying, and as liquids that can be sprayed directly. Granules are easier to apply, and most remain on the lawn longer than sprays, prolonging their effectiveness. In general, fungal diseases are difficult to control. If you know that a particular disease affects your lawn at a certain time of year, prevent it by applying the appropriate fungicide one to two weeks beforehand. Use fungicides with caution, and always study the product label, especially for rates and timing.

Pythium Blight (Grease Spot)
Treat with chemical controls when symptoms first appear. To prevent, water in the morning, avoid overwatering, and do not mow grass when wet.

Red Thread (Pink Patch)
Maintain an adequate nitrogen level and a soil pH of 6.5 to 7.0. Water in the morning. Control with appropriate fungicides.

Rust
To control, speed lawn growth with frequent fertilization and watering, then mow off infected leaves.

Summer Patch
To control, aerate, fertilize with a low-nitrogen formula, mow, and water correctly. An appropriate fungicide may also be used.

7 Identify cultural problems

Chemical burns caused by dog urine or spilled fertilizer, herbicides, or gasoline are characterized by distinct patches of dead grass sometimes surrounded by bright green growth. Drench urine and spilled fertilizers and herbicides with water. Where oil or gasoline have been spilled, drench with soapy water (the consistency of dishwater), then water thoroughly. The burned area can then be allowed to grow back, patched (see page 51), or reseeded.

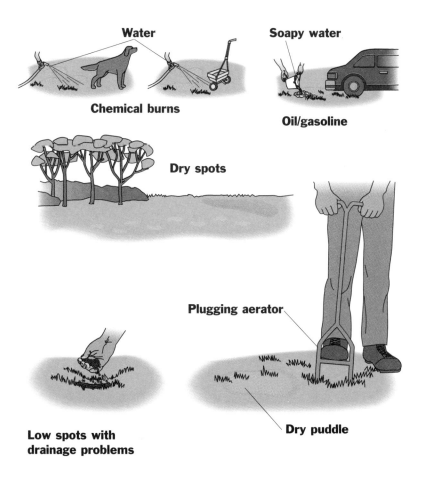

Water

Soapy water

Chemical burns

Oil/gasoline

Dry spots

Plugging aerator

Low spots with drainage problems

Dry puddle

If grass changes from bright to dull green, check the soil for moisture content—the lawn may be water starved. Low spots with drainage problems can be aerated or gradually filled in with more soil. Slightly yellowed lawns may need nitrogen or possibly iron fertilizer. Mowing a lawn too short (scalping) causes the exposed lower white portions of the grass blades to turn brown; mowing with dull blades gives a lawn a grayish cast a day or so later. Grass growing under trees can turn yellow from the shade or fallen leaves; thin out the trees and rake up the leaves.

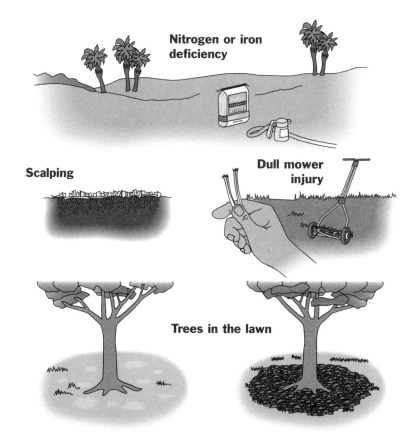

Nitrogen or iron deficiency

Scalping

Dull mower injury

Trees in the lawn

Renewing a Lawn

1 Aerate compacted soil

Aeration perforates the soil, allowing moisture and nutrients to penetrate better. Aerate clay soils once or twice a year; sandy soils once every year or two. Water the lawn well the day before. Use a motorized aerating machine or a foot-press aerator (both can be rented). Leave the plugs to dry for a day, then use a rake to break them up on top of the lawn, or mow and pulverize them, leaving the mower's discharge chute open without a grass-catcher bag. This creates a thin, beneficial top dressing. In heavy clay soils, rake up and discard the plugs.

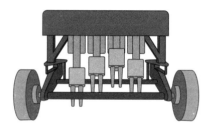

Aerator, with up-and-down motion

Aerate to remove cores or plugs of soil.

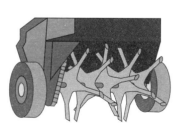

Aerator, with rotating motion

2 Dethatch thick layers

Thatch is a layer of slowly decomposing grass stems, dead roots, and debris that accumulates above the soil and below grass blades. Although a light layer of thatch can be beneficial, too much (more than ½ inch) can cause problems. Dethatching is a process of eradicating this buildup. It should be done every other year just prior to the most vigorous grass-growing season; in late spring for warm-season grasses and in late spring or early fall for cool-season grasses.

Too much thatch

Grass

Thatch

Roots and soil

2" plug of grass. Dethatch if the thatch layer is more than ¹/₂" thick.

Thatching rake

Vertical cutter

For small lawns, use a thatching rake. For larger areas (except in St. Augustine grass), use a dethatching machine, or vertical cutter. Set the tines to dig down ½ inch. The blades should completely penetrate the top half of the thatch layer and not disturb the soil. Go over the whole lawn, making parallel passes, then rake up and discard the loose thatch. Set the tines slightly lower and go over the entire lawn again at right angles to the first pass. Again, rake up and discard the thatch. Fertilize and water to help the lawn recover quickly.

Set the tines to dig down ½".

Rake up the loosened thatch.

Set the tines slightly lower and go over the lawn again at right angles to the first pass. Rake and discard thatch.

Overseed for green cover

3

Overseed a warm-season grass with a cool-season variety for a green lawn throughout the year. Use annual ryegrass or a prepackaged overseeding mix for best results. Start overseeding in late fall. If thatch isn't a problem, spread the seeds over the existing lawn and water them in. If thatch is heavy, mow close to the soil line (with a regular mower), rake up the clippings, then mow and rake again. Spread two to three times as much seed as you would for a new lawn over the existing lawn. Cover with ½ inch of topsoil or top dressing, and water.

Overseeding

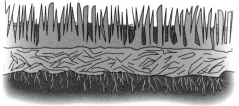

Overseeding in heavy thatch

Patch small spots

Restore damaged areas by reseeding or by removing the affected section and replacing it with a piece of sod. (Follow planting procedures on pages 14 through 19.) Dig out the damaged area with a shovel or trowel, loosen the top 3 to 6 inches of soil underneath, and replant. If spilled gasoline or herbicide caused the dead spot, remove several inches of the soil and replace it with untainted soil before planting. Keep patched areas watered and protected from foot traffic until established.

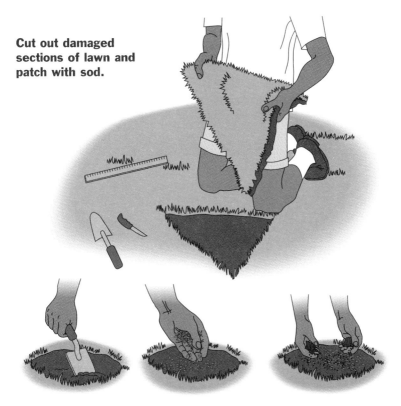

Cut out damaged sections of lawn and patch with sod.

To reseed, loosen soil. Fertilize, then level the soil. Spread seeds evenly—about 15 to 20 per square inch. Scratch seeds in, tamp them down, and smooth out soil. Add top dressing and keep the area moist.

5 Renovate a damaged lawn

To renovate a lawn that has undesirable grass types or has deteriorated badly, spray the old grass once or twice with the herbicide glyphosate to kill it. Remove as much of the old grass as possible so the new seed or sod will have good contact with the soil. If there is just a little thatch, slice through the dead material with a vertical cutter. Soil should be moist. Next, amend and level the soil, then replant with seeds, sod, sprigs, or plugs (see pages 14 to 19). Keep the newly renovated lawn well watered until it is established.

Use glyphosate to kill the old lawn.

Vertical-cut to remove thatch.

Rake up and discard debris.

If the layer of dead material and thatch is thicker than ¼ to ½ inch, use a flail dethatcher, setting it to cut to the soil level. After the machine finely chops the thatch material, rake it up and discard. Then slice the lawn with an over-seeder, slicer, or groover. Go over the lawn twice, the second time at a right angle to the first. The soil should be moist but not wet. After slicing the soil, amend and level it, then replant the lawn, keeping it well watered until established.

Moisten soil and aerate. Rake up soil cores and shred with a vertical cutter. Apply fertilizer. Plant seed or lay sod.

More Information

Lawn Shapes: How Many Square Feet?

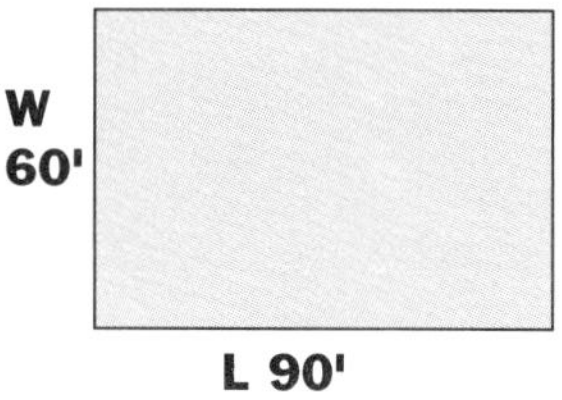

**W
60'**

L 90'

SQUARE OR RECTANGLE
Area = LW
L = Length
W = Width

For example: A = 90' × 60'
A = 5,400 square feet

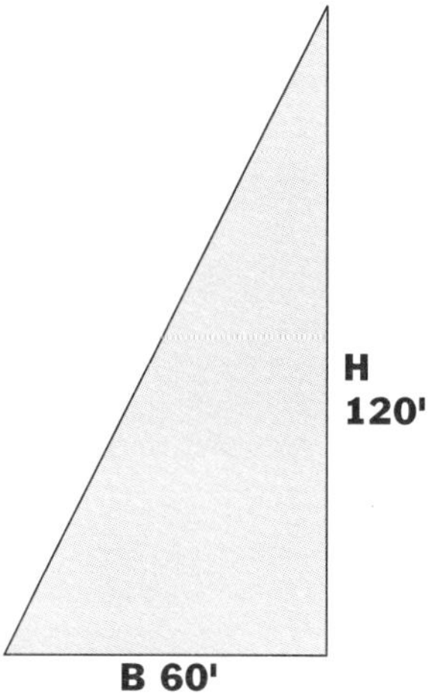

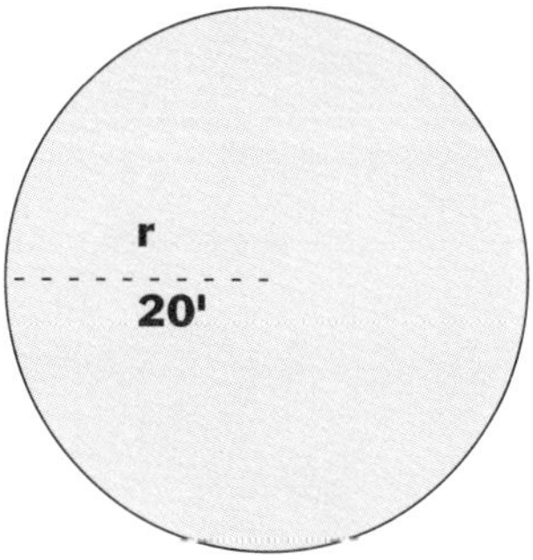

**r
20'**

**H
120'**

B 60'

CIRCLE
Area = πr^2
π = 3.14
r = Radius

For example:
A = 3.14 × 20' × 20'
A = 1,256 square feet

TRIANGLE
Area = 0.5 BH
B = Base
H = Height

For example:
A = 0.5 × 60' × 120'
A = 3,600 square feet

UNUSUAL SHAPES
Make calculations by
sections and total them.
In this example, calculate
these areas and add
figures together:
Area of triangle
Area of rectangle
$1/2$ area of circle
Total = square feet in area

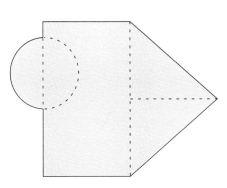

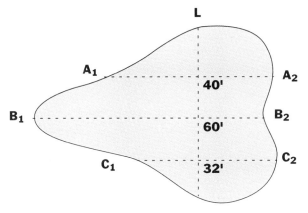

IRREGULAR SHAPES (accuracy within 5%)
Measure a length line (L) of the area. Every 10 feet
along the length line, measure the width at right angles
to the length line. Total the widths and multiply by 10.
Area = (A_1A_2 + B_1B_2 + C_1C_2 etc.) × 10'
A = (40' + 60' + 32') × 10'
A = 132' × 10'
A = 1,320 square feet

Lawn Grass Climates

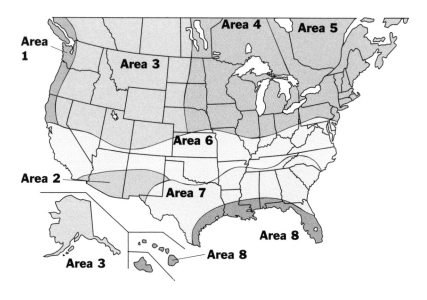

Best Lawn Grasses

Area 1: Cool-season bentgrass, Kentucky bluegrass, fine fescues, perennial ryegrass. Area 2: Bermudagrass, St. Augustine grass, and zoysiagrass. Where it's not too hot, try turf-type tall fescue. Area 3: Cool-season Kentucky bluegrass, fine fescues. Also try turf-type tall fescues and native grasses. Area 4: Cool-season bentgrass, Kentucky bluegrass, fine fescues, perennial ryegrass, and buffalograss; zoysiagrass in the southern portion of the area. Area 5: Bentgrass, fine fescues, Kentucky bluegrass, perennial ryegrass; zoysiagrass in southern Atlantic coastal areas. Area 6: Turf-type tall fescue, zoysiagrass, and cold-tolerant cultivars of bermudagrass. Area 7: Bermudagrass, centipedegrass, St. Augustine grass, and zoysiagrass. Use Kentucky bluegrass, fine fescues, turf-type tall fescue, and perennial ryegrass in cooler parts. Area 8: Bahiagrass, bermudagrass, centipedegrass, St. Augustine grass, and zoysiagrass.

Reading a Seed Label

This label is an example of what you find on grass seed boxes or containers. The proportions of grasses listed are only a sample. A good seed mixture is indicated by a low percentage of weed and crop seeds, an absence of noxious weeds, and high percentages of germination.

Fine-textured Grasses[1]	Origin[2]	Germination[3]
30% Kentucky bluegrass	Oregon	80%
20% 'Adelphi' Kentucky bluegrass	Oregon	80%
20% 'Fylking' Kentucky bluegrass	Oregon	80%
29% Creeping red fescue	Canada	90%
Coarse Kinds[4]	Other Ingredients	
None claimed	0.01% Crop seed[5]	
	1.05% Inert matter[6]	
	0.03% Weed seed[7]	
	No noxious weeds[8]	
Tested: No earlier than 9 months of date listed.[9]		

[1] Attractive lawns depend on fine-textured grasses. Look for common, high-quality grasses, such as Kentucky bluegrass and fine fescues. Named cultivars are considered superior to common types and, in most cases, are a sign of a good mixture. Percentages indicate the proportion of the grass by weight, not seed count.

[2] When seed quantities account for more than 5% of the mixture, the label must show the state or country where the seed crop was grown. This has no bearing on grass adaptation.

[3] Percentages represent the amount of seed that germinates under ideal conditions. Generally, the higher the percentage, the better.

[4] Generally, "coarse kinds" tend to clump and do not mix well with other grasses. Coarse-textured grasses should not exceed half of the mixture. The exception is turf-type perennial ryegrass.

[5] These are seeds from any commercially grown grass crop. Look for 0.00%.

[6] The chaff, dirt, and miscellaneous material that manages to escape cleaning is called inert matter. Although harmless, it should not total more than 3% to 4%.

[7] It is virtually impossible to keep all weed seeds out of a seed crop, but look for less than 1%.

[8] Noxious weeds are troublesome. A good seed mixture should have none.

[9] It is best to buy seed that shows a current date. Seed stored in a cool, dry place will last months longer than that date.

Mowing Heights

The following are recommended mowing heights for the most popular lawn grasses. In most areas and situations, a lawn will look good when mowed at any height within the range for its grass type.

Grass	Height in Inches
Cool-Season Grasses	
Bentgrass, Creeping	$1/4$–$3/4$
Bluegrass, Kentucky	$1\frac{1}{2}$–$2\frac{1}{2}$
Bluegrass, Rough	$1\frac{1}{2}$–2
Fescue, Chewings	1–$2\frac{1}{2}$
Fescue, Dwarf	$1\frac{1}{2}$–$2\frac{1}{2}$
Fescue, Hard	1–$2\frac{1}{2}$
Fescue, Red	$1\frac{1}{2}$–$2\frac{1}{2}$
Fescue, Tall	1–2
Ryegrass, Annual	$1\frac{1}{2}$–2
Ryegrass, Perennial	$1\frac{1}{2}$–2
Warm-Season Grasses	
Bahiagrass	2–3
Bermudagrass, Common	$3/4$–$1\frac{1}{2}$
Bermudagrass, Hybrid	$1/2$–1
Centipedegrass	1–2
St. Augustine Grass	$1\frac{1}{2}$–$2\frac{1}{2}$
Zoysiagrass	1–2
Native Grasses	
Blue Grama	2–3
Buffalograss	$2\frac{1}{2}$–3
Smooth Brome	3–6

Types of Grasses

Creeping bentgrass
Agrostis palustris
A cool-season grass; used extensively in cool climates for golf course putting greens and tees, lawn bowling greens, grass tennis courts, and some home lawns. Produces a fine-textured, soft, and very dense carpetlike lawn that must be carefully tended.

Kentucky bluegrass
Poa pratensis
A cool-season grass; blue-green in color, medium to fine textured, and very cold hardy, it is the most widely planted cool-season grass. Commonly used for athletic fields, golf fairways, and general-purpose lawns, but does require conscientious maintenance.

Rough bluegrass
Poa trivialis
A cool-season grass; bright green, fine textured, and shallow-rooted, with boat-shaped tips to its blades. Soft and cold hardy, it retains its color over winter in mild climates; is tolerant of moist soils and shade. Not as attractive as Kentucky bluegrass.

Chewings fescue
Festuca rubra commutata
A cool-season grass; aggressive, bunch-type fine fescue, sometimes used to overseed shady lawns, often in mixtures with perennial ryegrass; moderate wear tolerance; forms more thatch than other fine fescues.

Types of Grasses (continued)

Hard fescue
Festuca ovina var. *duriuscula*
A cool-season grass; tolerant of shade in well-drained soils, fairly drought resistant and salt tolerant; highly resistant to several diseases; stays green during extended dry periods. Grows in clumps and is slower to fill in than chewings and red fescue, but needs minimal maintenance when mature.

Red fescue
Festuca rubra
A cool-season grass; fine textured, with narrow, dark green blades, it grows well in both shade and drought—a frequent component of bluegrass mixtures; quite heat tolerant and not likely to form thatch; grows well on banks and slopes and looks especially lush when left unmowed.

Tall fescue
Festuca elatior (Festuca arundinacea)
A cool-season grass; good for home lawns, playing fields, and commercial grounds. Grows in sun or shade and stays green all year in mild-winter climates. Has a coarse texture and clumping style of growth. Popular turf-type dwarf fescues are quite drought resistant and require less mowing.

Annual ryegrass, Italian ryegrass
Lolium multiflorum
A cool-season grass; forms a medium- to coarse-textured lawn with moderate wear resistance; sometimes used as a temporary lawn in late spring in temperate climates; often used to overseed dormant warm-season grasses for winter color in mild-winter areas.

Types of Grasses (continued)

Perennial ryegrass
Lolium perenne
A cool-season grass; has deep green, glossy leaf blades. Has the best wear tolerance of any cool-season grass, but does not do well in extreme heat, cold, or drought—best adapted to coastal regions with mild winters and cool, moist summers, and will grow in full sun or partial shade.

Bahiagrass
Paspalum notatum
A warm-season grass; tough, coarse textured, and adapted to a wide range of soil conditions. Grown from the central coast of North Carolina to eastern Texas, and in central and southwestern Florida, bahiagrass does best where rainfall is regular and plentiful. It needs frequent mowing.

Common bermudagrass
Cynodon dactylon
A warm-season grass; fine to medium textured; has deep roots that help make it heat and drought tolerant (although it looks better if given adequate water). Invasive by nature— keep it out of areas where it is not wanted. It does not grow well in shade, and goes dormant in fall or winter in cool climates.

Hybrid bermudagrass
Cynodon species
A warm-season grass; softer, denser, and finer textured than common bermudagrass; fast-growing, durable, and heat-loving, it is used for home lawns and golf courses. Fairly drought tolerant, but looks better if given more water. Needs frequent mowing, quite a bit of fertilizer, and full sun.

Types of Grasses (continued)

Centipedegrass
Eremochloa ophiuroides
A warm-season grass; coarse textured, light green; grown mostly in the Southeast and Hawaii. Adapts to poor soil, is aggressive enough to crowd out weeds, and requires less mowing than other grasses. It is one of the first warm-season grasses to turn brown during extended hot, dry periods.

St. Augustine grass
Stenotaphrum secundatum
A warm-season grass; robust and fast-growing; coarse textured with broad, dark green blades. Among the most shade tolerant of the warm-season grasses. Tolerant of salt sprays, salty soil, and heat. Requires frequent watering and tends to lose its color when it gets cold.

Zoysiagrass
Zoysia species
A warm-season grass; tolerant of heat and drought yet able to endure some shade. Forms a dense, wiry, fine-textured lawn that crowds out weeds. Its needlelike blades can be sharp underfoot. Does not thrive where summers are short or cool; it goes dormant sooner than other warm-season grasses and may stay brown longer.

Soil Amendments

Organic Matter: Cubic Yards to Add*

Cubic Yards to Add to 6" of Soil to Achieve
Desired Percentage of Organic Matter

Area in Square Feet	10%	15%	20%	25%	30%
300	0.6	0.8	1.1	1.4	1.7
500	0.9	1.4	1.9	2.3	2.8
1,000	1.9	2.8	3.7	4.6	5.6
3,000	5.6	8.3	11.1	13.9	16.7
5,000	9.3	13.9	18.5	23.1	27.8
10,000	18.5	27.8	37.0	46.3	55.6
20,000	37.0	55.6	74.1	92.6	111.1
40,000	74.1	111.1	148.1	185.2	222.2

Ground Limestone: Amounts to Raise Soil pH to 6.5

Pounds to Add (per 1,000 square feet)**

Original pH	Sand	Sandy Loam	Loam	Silt Loam	Clay Loam
4.0	60	115	161	193	230
4.5	51	96	133	161	193
5.0	41	78	106	129	152
5.5	28	60	78	92	106
6.0	14	32	41	51	55

Soil Sulfur: Amounts to Lower Soil pH to 6.5

Pounds to Add (per 1,000 square feet)

Original pH	Sand	Sandy Loam	Loam	Silt Loam	Clay Loam
8.5	46	51	57	63	69
8.0	28	31	34	40	46
7.5	11	14	18	20	23
7.0	2	3	4	5	7

*One cubic yard covers 162 square feet to a depth of 2".
**In the southern and coastal states, reduce the application by approximately one half.

U.S./Metric Conversions

Formulas for Exact Measures

Rounded Measures for Quick Reference

	Symbol	When you know:	Multiply by:	To find:	Rounded Measures for Quick Reference
Mass (Weight)	oz	ounces	28.35	grams	1 oz = 30 g
	lb	pounds	0.45	kilograms	4 oz = 115 g
	g	grams	0.035	ounces	8 oz = 225 g
	kg	kilograms	2.2	pounds	16 oz = 1 lb = 450 g
					32 oz = 2 lb = 900 g
					36 oz = $2^1/_4$ lb = 1000 g (1 kg)
Volume	pt	pints	0.47	liters	1 c = 8 oz = 250 ml
	qt	quarts	0.95	liters	2 c (1pt) = 16 oz = 500 ml
	gal	gallons	3.785	liters	4 c (1 qt) = 32 oz = 1 liter
	ml	milliliters	0.034	fluid ounces	4 qt (1 gal) = 128 oz = $3^3/_4$ liter
Length	in.	inches	2.54	centimeters	$^3/_8$ in. = 1.0 cm
	ft	feet	30.48	centimeters	1 in. = 2.5 cm
	yd	yards	0.9144	meters	2 in. = 5.0 cm
	mi	miles	1.609	kilometers	$2^1/_2$ in. = 6.5 cm
	km	kilometers	0.621	miles	12 in. (1 ft) = 30.0 cm
	m	meters	1.094	yards	1 yd = 90.0 cm
	cm	centimeters	0.39	inches	100 ft = 30.0 m
					1 mi = 1.6 km
Temperature	° F	Fahrenheit	$^5/_9$ (after subtracting 32)	Celsius	32° F = 0° C
	° C	Celsius	$^9/_5$ (then add 32)	Fahrenheit	212° F = 100° C
Area	in.^{2}	square inches	6.452	square centimeters	1 in.^{2} = 6.5 cm^2
	ft^2	square feet	929.0	square centimeters	1 ft^2 = 930 cm^2
	yd^2	square yards	8361.0	square centimeters	1 yd^2 = 8360 cm^2
	a.	acres	0.4047	hectares	1 a. = 4050 m^2